ANNAPOLIS E. SHAW

To Live

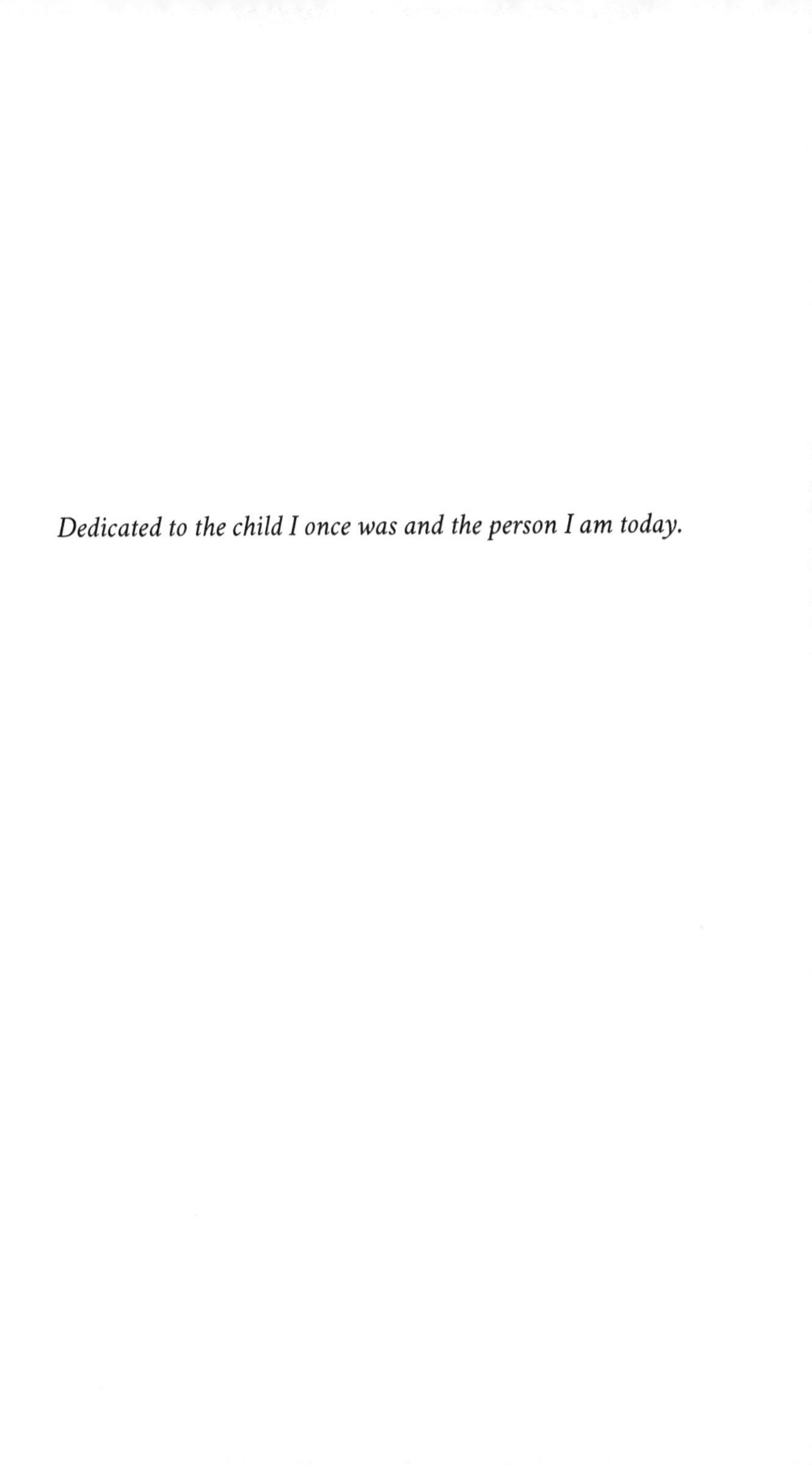

Dedicated to the child I once was and the person I am today.

"You could write a book one day."

Nellie Ann Robinson

Contents

Acknowledgement

Inspired by Amanda Lovelace, Rupi Kaur, Nayyirah Waheed, and other poets who use this art modernly, whilst courageously breaking the boundaries of what poetry is and can be.

Thank you to my loving husband, for proofreading and editing this during the creation of my story.

1

Rebirth

and somehow
   i found myself in dresses
   when years ago
   i was covering my body
   due to self-made scars

— time does heal.

2

Mother

there was one
  then two
  then three
  three
  minus one
  equals two

when my brother died
  your mind died with him
  and one day
  you lost it on me

— i always wonder if you love me still.

3

Name Change

you named me
    to spite the man
    that gave life to me

you tore me down
    creating scars
    that i will forever see

now i step into the courthouse
    paperwork in hand
    to change the name you gave to me
    to undo the spite
    you wanted for him
    creating a new life, you see

— why did you name me like this?

4

Evolution

Kindred to a
   Disaster
   and
   Manufactured
   Ridiculously
   Justified

And
   Escaped now
   She

— i escaped and i do not love you.

5

POTS Syndrome

i fainted
  haphazardly
  from your room you ran to me

unfortunately
  these times
  were the only times you cared for me

— you only loved me when i was sick.

6

444

four times one
   four times one
   and four times one again

i see you
   on billboards
   on apartments
   on mailboxes

emerging from heaven

— God is always with me.

7

It Must Be Destiny

october fourteenth
  was the day
  you gave your life to me

the day you danced
  in my body
  spreading your desire
  inside of me

the following day
  you would say
  how much you loved me

and to this day
  you still say
  it must be destiny

— marriage is not hard, it is teamwork.

8

Lexapro

and so
    i popped that pill that morning
    feeling the happiest
    i'd ever been
    not understanding
    why it was that i
    couldn't feel that way
    on my own

— i understand why my patients call it a happy pill now.

9

Nana

and one night
  in your backseat
  i voiced
  that i liked the idea
  of dissipation

you suggested instead
  eradication

and i almost went home
  and preformed
  self mutilation

— this would be the first time, but not the last time, that i
thought about this.

10

BANG!

BANG!
  was the sound
  of my skull
  slamming
  against tile covered concrete

with enough force
  to break
  the bones
  in my nose
  and my maxilla

— nose goes.

11

Sad, sad, girl

sometimes
  i wonder
  privately
  silently
  frightfully
  spitefully
  if i deserved what you did to me

or if
  i was meant
  to be a sad, sad, girl

— you both hurt me so, so much.

12

Archangel

you welcomed me
   into your sanctuary
   and terrified
   of what religion
   i would be invited to

i played hard to catch

in around six months
   you baptized me
   and i walked into your temple
   ready to serve you
   praise you
   love you

in around two years
   i was excommunicated
   and the reason
   you say

is because you loved the idea of me
and never loved me

— the devil was once an angel too.

13

Sorority

as a child
   i was never one to fit in
   i was not blonde
   blue eyed
   nor skinned tanned-colored
   like beautiful beachy sands

instead
   i was brunette
   brown eyed
   and skinned cocoa-colored
   like soft earthy soils

since then
   i found myself
   desiring to look
   like the sand-colored girls
   with their ocean blue eyes

because
    maybe then
    i will finally fit in

                              15

and join
    a sorority
    and be considered
    beautiful then

— i want to join a sorority.

14

The Devil Saved Me

and there i was
    pinned down
    giving you
    every inch of me

arms behind my back
    expecting the pain to stop
    allowing you
    to fulfill your desire
    while the devil watched over

but for some reason
    the devil had to save me
    why is it
    that even he saw
    that you were hurting me
    that day

— why couldn't you see how rough you were.

15

I Hate My Hair

my hair falls—
  well not falls
  it
  s
  t
  a
  n
  d
  s
  defying gravity
  unmanaged
  unprofessional
  too coarse
  too short
  unkempt
  incorrect
  and this
  is what made me hate it

— i constantly change my hair still.

16

Trichotillomania

pluck one
   pluck two
   pluck three

lose one
   lose two
   lose three

as my eyelashes perish
   whisked away by the wind
   i cannot resist the urge
   to pluck still

— i wish to get better at this.

17

Podcast

i made myself a safe space
  a sacred space
  a cozy place

a place where i can feel your grace
  a place where i can see your face
  and God
  i dedicate this podcast to you
  in hopes
  i'll get into heaven too

— will i see my brother again someday?

18

I Tribute Myself to You

presently
  i look quite like my younger self
  with the same brand mascara
  with the same styled clothes
  with the same permed hair
  and the same white colored toes

consequently
  i often wonder
  was this version of myself
  the version i was supposed to be
  before i lost my mind?

— was that the best version of 'me'?

19

Baptized

i fell back into the water
    bowed down
    by my pastor
    pastor's friends
    pastor's family

but not only
    did i bow down
    to the summerish water
    i bowed down
    to faith
    to praise
    to grace
    to you
    oh, God

but in bowing down
    and submitting myself
    into summerish water

i submitted
my sins
to You

23

— i didn't feel this way when i was baptized the first time.

20

Tongues

i always admired
  my husband
  for being able to speak in Tongues

until one day
  i spoke in a language
  that was only native
  to You

— TOP saved me.

21

G*ddamn

and here i am
    saying the one curse word
    i vowed not to say
    as it vains' your name

disrespecting your pain

and i continue to wonder
    am i the same?
    from before
    i gave my life
    to You

— i need to go to church.

22

Happy Feet

did you know that i saved you?
   from a mother
   whose cannibalistic idea
   was to tear your limbs
   one by one
   two by two
   and sacrifice you?

did you know that you saved me?
   from a mother
   whose sadistic idea
   was to destroy my mind
   vein by vein
   tissue by tissue
   and commit child abuse?

— i love you like you are my child.

23

Myrder

you had a younger sister
  but
  we murdered her
  on a drunken night
  throwing a "birthday bash"

when the only thing that bashed
  was my head
  against the dash
  before the airbags went off
  and i totaled her

— we have you now.

24

Snow

i went to the mountains
    last year
    in hopes i'd see
    snow

its glistening tears
    which fall
    from dove colored clouds

i wonder if
    my tears are this beautiful
    too

— i still haven't seen more than a couple inches of snow.

25

Lavender

and that night
  i asked him
  "if i were a color,
  what color would i be?"
  and he said
  "lavender."

and in that moment
  i imagined
  lavender flowers
  blowing softly
  in the springtime wind
  in a beautiful field
  where the sun glows
  delicately

— does he view me like this?

26

Anorexia

i remember in middle school
   i was a track and field
   superstar

i ran like the wind
   glided like a squirrel
   flew like an eagle
   and jumped like a frog

but i was much skinnier then
   not skinnier—
   frailer
   more delicate
   unhealthy

and in high school
   i thought to myself
   when i ended in last place
   for the first time

how could i
run like the wind
glide like a squirrel
fly like an eagle
and jump like a frog?

and now
i was a different type of
superstar

i was best
at counting calories
shotgunning creatine
weighing fat
and crying silently

i still ended up in last place
and not only on the field
i ended up last

with wounds unhealed

— i quit track after i got Rhabdomyolysis.

27

Witch

all of my life
   i noticed the "what if"
   in things

"what if" i was a mermaid
   "what if" i was a werewolf
   "what if" i was a vampire
   "what if" i was a witch

presently in life
   i often wonder if i used these things
   labels
   creatures
   species
   to run away from the fact that i am
   human

with flaws i still have to accept

28

Arrested

the night i was arrested
  i finally understood
  racism
  sexism
  sadism
  absolutism

and how important it is
  to participate in activism

see,
  the night they detained me
  i had just turn nineteen
  not understanding

why they were bullying me

— i was arrested for a crime i did not commit.

29

Darby

every day
   i walk by your grave
   but i don't go visit

because the thought of visiting your lifeless body
   pains me too much

— you were the first pet that i truly ever loved.

30

Motivation

every day
  i find myself losing more
  and more
  motivation

i cannot do my hair
  i cannot brush my teeth
  i cannot make my bed
  i cannot simply breathe

because
  depression
  you are choking me
  and strangling the motivation
  directly out of me

— i did not used to be like this.

31

Butterflies

you told me
   after you said your vows that day
   you've never felt butterflies
   in that way

and from that moment
   i admired you more
   because
   your kaleidoscope
   had been born

— it is so courageous, so normal, and so beautiful that men experience "butterflies".

32

You are Allowed to Cry

honey
    you are allowed to cry
    and allowed to show fear
    and allowed to show pain
    and allowed to be "weak"

and honey
    that doesn't make you any less masculine
    or any less of what "a man" is supposed to be
    if anything
    that's what makes you so endearing
    to me

— men are allowed to have emotions.

33

Voice

my voice
  is my gift
  from God

— i hope you find yours too.

34

Magic

i used to turn to magic
   for my troubles
   my fears
   my money issues
   my tears

but then i gave my life to You
   and discovered
   that God's magic
   is true

— i love you God.

35

Amnesia

i lost you
   one day
   somehow
   someway
   is this why i named you
   Amnesia?

— Amnesia was my favorite childhood rag-doll.

36

Brothers' Grave

you lie there
    cold
    and alone

and on holidays
    and on birthdays

and each day
    and every night

and even then
    i still refuse
    to go see you

— i refuse to see him like this.

37

Childish Hairstyles

why is it that
   i am more attractive
   not with my natural hair
   but with hairstyles
   that are straight

or with ponytails
   and with bows

why is it
   that society
   likes
   childish hairstyles

— am i a grown woman.

38

Knives and Pens

and momma
    when you ran
    at me
    with a knife
    that day

i arrived
    at school
    in hopes
    that my counselor's pen
    would scribble down
    what you did to me

and instead
    we had CPS come
    for the next five years
    and at night
    you still threatened
    to kill me

— "you better not go to sleep tonight."

39

Sexuality

you could say i was confused
    or misused
    or induced

when it comes
    to my sexuality

but one things for sure
    and two thing's for certain

i didn't
    consent
    to being
    this way

— i was a child.

40

The Dominate Root

once you eliminate
   the dominate root
   the roots around them
   will eliminate themselves

— trauma.

41

Bipolar Disorder

as a child
  i wished to have
  bipolar disorder
  because maybe then
  i'd get the attention
  i would not
  receive at home

and when i got it
  i realized
  just how true
  the saying is
  to be careful
  just exactly
  what you wish
  for

— being bipolar is the worst thing that has ever happened to
me.

42

Piercings

to my nose
   i say sorry
   for puncturing you
   not once
   not twice
   but three times through

simply
   because
   i was embarrassed
   of you

to my tongue
   i say sorry
   for penetrating you
   only once
   but that
   was too many times
   too

i find
   that i tend
   to pierce my body
   when i can't
   pierce my mind
   with solitude

— physical pain numbs mental pain.

43

Violin Strings

and the sound
   of violin strings
   resemble the melody
   of what song
   i want my soul
   to sing

— i am growing into a softer woman.

44

Artist

and i found myself
  in art again
    after many moons

of abandonment

— art block.

45

Self-harm

they say that
  scars
  tell a story
  but these scars
  the scars
  that i inflicted
  upon myself

tell a time
  where i wanted
  my story
  to end

—seven years clean.

46

Bible

most times
   we ask ourselves
   how exactly
   do we hear God

yet
   he gave us a book
   with his voice
   right there

— open your Bible.

47

Father(less)

the day
   you bruised
   my eyes
   my forehead
   my lips
   with firm
   folded
   newspaper

i screamed
   to my mother
   "save me"
   "SAVE ME"

but
   she still
   had to save
   herself

— something changed in her that day.

55

48

Piano Tiles

you dragged me
   across the floor
   like fingers
   on piano tiles

C
  D
  E
  F

G
  A
  B
  C

and then i hit a note
   that was incorrect
   unpleasant
   sharp

on a piano
  we call it
   "D Sharp"

but on my body
  we call it
   "my head"

— *ow.*

49

Domestic Violence

there was one night
  where he had thrown you
  so hard
  against my bed frame
  that you seized
  me uneased
  our minds diseased

with the thought
  that your life
  would be ceased

— i thought we were going to die.

50

My Mother Told Me She Hated Me

i was lying in bed
   the night you told me you hated me

i replayed what you said
   the night you told me you hated me

and i wished i was dead
   the night you told me you hated me

— i was six years old.

51

Give Me Up

and one night
  you said to me
  that if my brother were alive
  you would
  give
  me
  u
  p

and at that age
  i truly believed
  that you would sign those papers
  and abandon me

— you threatened to leave me countless times after this.

52

Punch Buggy

no punch back
  at least
  those are the rules right?

until you actually
  punched me in the back
  and my teacher
  found that bruise
  on me

— i became acquainted with CPS after this.

52

53

Russian Roulette

one gun
  two fates

one live
  one blank

so i picked up the gun
  pointing it
  to the sun

where surprisingly
  it unloaded
  a dud

one gun
  one fate

one live
  no blanks

then you picked up the gun
   pointing it
   to my mug

and you smiled
   because you knew
   you won

— i would have hurt myself before hurting you, but you didn't
feel the same, momma.

54

Jumped

he crawled
    into our back door
    wearing a body
    that screamed
    "assault"

there was blood from his head
    bruises on his eyes
    blood from his nose
    and swelling on his lips

he reminded me
    of myself that day

— my mother often chose the wrong men.

55

Hand Gun

in our kitchen
   i remember screaming
   mother being demeaning
   hand gun
   slightly gleaming

and at that moment
   i wished i were dreaming
   because i witnessed
   a man
   almost take
   his own life

— click click, but no bang.

56

Bushes and Blue Skies

i remember
    looking to the sky
    as i fell into the bushes

pushed forcefully
    by my own
    grandmother

i was not pushed
    rather i was—
    slammed
    down violently
    with her hand
    'round my throat

— the sky was pretty that day.

57

I Am Not Your Type

why is it
  that men
  that i attempt to be friends with
  fail to recognize
  that i
  am
  not
  their type

— i just want genuine friendship.

58

Clothing Hanger

on your place of rest
  i asked for a dress
  wanting only
  to look
  my best

and you told me "no"
  and i wanted to go
  as far
  as to ask
  for a "yes"

and to my surprise
  i couldn't believe my eyes
  a hanger
  began running
  towards me

and when it finally stopped

the feeling
it was hot
as it decided
to
strike me

— my stomach welted for two days and two nights after this.

59

Thin Walls

one day
  my mother informed me
  that my father
  threw my body
  against
  the apartment's wall

though i vaguely remember
  i do have to consider
  if i
  was the reason
  for that mysterious hole

— 11:11.

60

Snap (Beans)

have you ever heard of snap beans?
   those things
   that make sounds
   like
   snap
   crackle
   pop?

well,
   my mind
   made those sounds

not long after
   something vicious
   had snapped
   inside of me

— "snapping" is a real thing.

61

My Mother Told Me to Tell You That I Hate You

i stood
    atop the couch
    in the mirror
    hung closest
    to your R&B
    CD
    stand

filled with Micheal Jackson
    Whitney Houston
    and Marvin Gaye

i'm curious
    if they heard me
    that day

as my words bounced harshly
    off paper thin walls

heart drumming
    as i made
    this call

73

i shouted *"**I HATE YOU**"*
    and though encouraged
    i cried
    because him and i
    died
    inside

— my father did not deserve to hear this.

62

Cold Nights

and on cold nights
  i hold you
  so tight

that i believe
  our souls
  touch

— i love you.

63

Thailand

my dream
   is to go
   to Thailand

no,
   my dream
   is to *live*
   in Thailand

and maybe finally
   i will get to see
   the wonder
   of living
   in my fantasy

— exit stage left.

64

Peek-a-boo!

i see you!
　or—
　i *seen* you

where did you go
　father?

— you tend to pop into and out of my life.

65

Hot in the Pants

the weather was cold
  when he asked me
  if i
  were hot
  in the pants

and my legs did a dance
  while my mind did handstands

wondering why
  i seemed hot
  in the pants

— you say you never said this, but i remember.

66

Boy Parts

i walked in
   and he was there
   boy parts
   standing tall
   in the air

mother shielded my eyes
   but there i still cried
   and for the first time
   i wished
   i had died

— cooties.

67

Domestic Violence 2

my mother
  screamed
  and screamed
  and screamed
  and screamed
  at a person
  who was never mean

over years of being battered
  my mother
  had gathered
  that "if i scream
  they can't scream
  at me"

— she began abusing people who meant no harm.

68

Porn Addict

i held his phone
  black cased
  history erased
  and i
  staring down
  pale faced

there was ecstasy on her face
  mind a waste
  insides caked
  with his
  icing
  smearing over
  her base

— i learned what semen was that day.

69

Smelling Green

a light
   came on
   and a jar
   came with it
   you submerged
   my nose
   in green

but what's
   inside?
   could it get
   me high?
   dear god,
   i can bare-
   ly breathe

— after this, i still didn't know what marijuana was.

70

Death Song

and we danced
  and we danced
  and danced
  and danced
  to a song
  chanting lyrics
  of your death

for i pictured the depth
  of your final breath
  yet somehow
  with the Lord
  you were kept

— my mother survived six fibroid tumors and fibroid cysts the
size of baseballs.

71

Good

and when you came back
   the last time
   you *knew*
   you were mistreating me

and sometimes
   you would say
   "good"
   or
   "im proud of you"
   when i told you
   "no"

— narcissist.

72

Love is Patient

love is patient
  love is kind
  but it can also
  make hearts
  go blind

but when i let <u>you</u>
  in my mind
  i learned that

love *is* patient
  and love *is* kind

— my love for you resembles the color pink.

73

Amateur Cheerleader

i've always
  wanted
    to be a cheerleader

and eventually
  i did
    become one

but instead
  of cheering
    for a team

i cheered
  to raise
    my self esteem

— when you have no support group, you support yourself.

74

Brothers' Mobile

we hung up
  my brothers' mobile
  shortly after
  he died

and the music
  still makes
  me cry

though i understand
  God had the upper hand

i can't help
  but to wonder
  why?

— why was he taken from us?

75

Bitter Ballerina

i was laid
    on your chest
    when you went
    on your quest
    to the place
    we all
    know best

though
    when you died
    you left back
    a lullaby
    and when the ballerina
    dances
    she cries

— a pink, ballerina music box.

76

Marine Sunsets

how could someone
    look outside
    and think
    there is
    no God?

— look at the oceans and sunsets.

76

77

Maroon Cowboy

and one day
 my mother
 gave me
 a hat

a cowboy hat
 a without joy
 hat

for this
 is the hat
 that you left me

and i wonder
 in heaven
 have you been
 set free?

— yeehaw.

Imposter Syndrome

i often wonder
   if i'm doing enough
   if i'm pursuing enough
   if i'm not enough

but i'm doing too much

— i'm tired of not being pleased with myself.

79

Skin-and-Bones

growing up
  i was always told
  that i resembled
  skin and bones

"Ethiopia child"
  "malnourished child"
  "you're starving, child"
  "what happened, my child?"

but in the end
  she failed to realize
  that this was the result
  of being marginalized

— If a child is undergoing mental stress, the body cannot be healthy.

80

Jury Judy

i participated
   in a youth
   justice system

and i anticipated
   the difference
   i could make

i was excited
   to weed out the bad
   emphasize the good
   punish the criminal
   and bring back brotherhood

but
   often
   i wonder
   why
   the adult justice system

couldn't save me
from my household

— my mother broke my nose and they gave her a warning.

81

Flimsy

back when i did gymnastics
  my
  "flexibility"
  was a gift
  from God

wondrous
  talented
  extraordinary

but now
  this same
  "flexibility"
  is the reason i cannot climb stairs

— Ehlers Danlos Syndrome.

82

Oreo

you know the saying
   too black to be white
   but
   too white to be black?

well unfortunately
   i struggle with that

i will never know
   if
   i will find my place

can someone
   please
   give me a safe space?

— "you're the whitest black girl i have ever seen."

83

Sorrowful Soldier

at one point
  i wanted to be a soldier

Flight Nurse
  Air Force Reserves

until i discovered
  that i was
  bipolar

momma,
  why did you traumatize me?

— crushed dreams.

84

Blessings Upon Blessings

when you give someone blessings
  they come back
  ten fold

to give someone a blessing
  is not something
  to withhold

— "do unto others as you would have them do unto you." -
Matthew 7:12

85

Premature Prodigy

you could've
  called me
  a premature
  prodigy

young
  intelligent
  talented

until my illness
  came and haunted me

— i lost touch with my gifts when i became depressed.

86

Laced

"open your mouth"
   she said to me
   as the clear
   ripe liquid
   was sprayed
   onto my tongue

there was a bitter taste
   then a bitter feeling
   then regret was on her face

when she realized what she'd done

— i was a gullible child.

Battlefield

there's not a single battle
  that was fought
  with one man
  and if they did
  they were slain

— there is a God.

88

Divine Radiance

and suddenly
   the radiance
   of God
   was flowing
   through my bloodstream

— the light of God shines through me.

89

Age like Fine Wine

and today
  i realized
  how beautiful
  my patients' smiles were

the life in their eyes
  the lines in their smile
  and the gentleness of their voices

if only
  i could be as angelic as them one day

— aging is beautiful.

90

Cash Cow

i don't understand
   how one day
   i became the one you ask for money from
   when at first
   i was less fortunate than you

— stop asking me for money.

91

Acceptance

and suddenly
    i was accepted
    by everyone
    when at first
    i was deemed
    a no one

— sister, sister.

92

Survival vs Living

there's something freeing
   about doing the things
   you want to do
   with no anxiety
   no pain
   no anger
   no shame

there is a difference
   between survival
   versus
   living

— do it.

93

Youthful Eye bags

there is beauty
  in being exhausted
  because then you know
  you are living your life
  to the fullest
  every day

— i am tired but i am alive.

93

Knock-Out

and for some reason
  you asked me
  to wrestle
  a man
  that was far
  out
  of my weight-class

in this boxing ring
  i was the only one
  that received
  blows

— why did you put me in harms way?

94

95

Brain Game

the brain
   is a wonderful
   colorful
   powerful
   place
   that we often
   discard
   due to
   wasted
   potential

— you only use around 10% of our brain.

96

I Love You Too

as a child
  i struggled
  with finding
  comfort
  in saying
  "i love you too"

because
  my mother
  never said
  "i love you"

— "we don't say that here."

97

Gravesite

my grandfather
   allowed me to pick
   my great uncle's
   gravesite

and there was flowers
   and trees
   and emerald grass
   and lively things

but
   why is it
   that everything was alive
   but him?

— the nature showed how beautiful you were.

98

Apology

my father
   took it upon himself
   to apologize
   for everything
   he had done to me

and
   as his daughter
   i forgave him

and the only reason
   i cannot forgive you
   mother
   is because
   he changed
   and you did not

— same ole' same ole'

99

Self-worth

i now realize
   that to be kind
   is to be beautiful
   and there is nothing

that clothing
   makeup
   and hair
   can fix
   if there is evil
   within your soul

— beauty *does* come from the inside.

99

100

To Live

and one day
   she started
   To Live

— thank you for reading.